PARENT'S GUIDE TO THE GEORGIA CRCT* FOR GRADE 3

Cynthia and Drew Johnson

Simon & Schuster

NEW YORK · LONDON · SINGAPORE · SYDNEY · TORONTO

*Criterion-Referenced Competency Tests

Kaplan Publishing
Published by Simon & Schuster
1230 Avenue of the Americas
New York, NY 10020

Copyright © 2001 by Anaxos, Inc.

All rights reserved. No part of this book may be reproduced or transmitted in any form or by any means, electronic or mechanical, including photocopying, recording, or by any information storage and retrieval system, without the written permission of the publisher, except where permitted by law.

Kaplan® is a registered trademark of Kaplan, Inc.

For bulk sales to schools, colleges, and universities, please contact: Order Department, Simon & Schuster, 100 Front Street, Riverside, NJ 08075. Phone: 1-800-223-2336. Fax: 1-800-943-9831.

All of the practice questions in this book were created by the authors to illustrate question types. They are not actual test questions. The material in this book is up-to-date at the time of publication. However, the Georgia Department of Education may have instituted changes in the test after this book was published. For more information on the CRCT, visit the Georgia Department of Education's Website at www.doe.k12state.ga.us.

Project Editor: Megan Duffy
Contributing Editor: Marc Bernstein, Marcy Bullmaster, and Phillip Vlahakis
Cover Design: Cheung Tai
Interior Page Design: Gumption Design
Production Editor: Maude Spekes
Editorial Coordinator: Déa Alessandro
Production Manager: Michael Shevlin
Executive Editor: Del Franz

Special thanks to: Rudy Robles

Manufactured in the United States of America

September 2001

10 9 8 7 6 5 4 3 2 1

ISBN 0-7432-0494-8

CONTENTS

Acknowledgments	vi
Introduction	vii
Chapter One: The A's, B's, C's, and D's of Good Test Taking	1
Chapter Two: Reading	11
Chapter Three: Mathematics	21
Chapter Four: English/Language Arts	33
Chapter Five: Science and Social Studies	39
Chapter Six: I Got a What?!	47
Chapter Seven: Math and Reading Practice	49

Acknowledgments

The authors would like to thank Maureen McMahon, Lori DeGeorge, and Megan Duffy for their enormous contributions towards making this book a reality.

INTRODUCTION

Although several years have passed since you were eight years old, your third-grade experience is probably not very different from your child's. There are still spelling bees at school, dodgeball games at recess, and giggling fits during class in which students try to stop laughing, but just can't. These are all memories you can share with your child. However, the memory of spending time in intensive preparation for a series of standardized tests is one your child will have all on his own.

The tests in question are part of the Georgia's Criterion-Referenced Competency Tests, or CRCT. The third-grade exams, which are scheduled to debut in Spring 2002, will be similar to the CRCT currently administered to all Georgia fourth-, sixth-, and eighth-graders. (At press time, legislature was being passed that would implement the tests in all grades, from first through eighth.) The CRCT are actually three different multiple-choice–only tests given to students in the subjects of Reading, Mathematics, and English/Language Arts (ELA). Students in grades three through eight will also have the pleasure of taking a Science test and a Social Studies test beginning in 2002.

Each subject test is given in two sessions lasting 45–60 minutes apiece. The Math CRCT contains the most questions (60), while the Reading test includes just 40 questions. Your child will also see 50 English/Language Arts questions. Critics of the CRCT could state that some IRS forms are easier to understand than these test formats. While this might be true, if you and your child take the time to familiarize yourselves with the test structure, your child will not be confused or frustrated by the test format, and will instead approach the exam experience with the confidence of a veteran accountant handling a 1040EZ form.

> **Calling All Students!**
>
> While only fourth-, sixth-, and eight-graders presently take these tests, a plan is in place to prescribe the Reading, Math, and ELA CRCT to all Georgia students from grades one through eight, beginning in 2002. Furthermore, as of 2002, two additional CRCT exams, Science and Social Studies, will be given to grades three through eight.

How the CRCT Were Born

A little history will help put these tests in perspective. In 1997, the Georgia Department of Education (GDOE) introduced an updated curriculum framework called the Quality Core Curriculum. These standards discussed what students should know in such core areas as

English, math, science, and social science. The CRCT program was then created to test these new standards, and to see how well students were learning these subjects. The effects of the higher standards were shown in the results from the first wave of students who took this new test (the CRCT debuted in 2000): Only 65 percent of all Georgia fourth graders, for example, received a passing score on the Reading exam, and just 62 percent received an acceptable grade on the Math test. The children did fare a little better on the ELA CRCT, with 71 percent receiving a passing score. These failure rates made headlines statewide and, understandably, caused widespread concern (and finger pointing) among parents and educators. Some critics claim the test is too hard, others that the students are poorly prepared. The debate continues.

Though the dust has yet to settle, one thing seems clear: Low scores do not mean these tests will be made easier or eliminated. The emphasis on standardized testing at all levels is growing stronger, not weaker. With "accountability" the pervasive theme in national education, more and more states are setting academic standards and then rewarding or punishing schools depending on whether they achieve these standards.

What's at Stake?

With so much emphasis being placed on the CRCT, you'd think the third graders who take them should be given the right to vote as a reward (at least in state elections). Quite a bit is at stake, for both the child and the school district. Based on test performance, the state ranks all schools based on how well or how poorly their students fared on the exam. Low-performing schools face the possibility of having superintendents, principals, or teachers fired (although for now there is no specific plan in place to deal with such schools). As for the individual third grader, at the time of this book's publication, Georgia lawmakers put the wheels in motion to make the this new third-grade CRCT a "high stakes test"—meaning that beginning in the spring of 2004, all third graders statewide will have to pass the reading portion of the CRCT to be promoted to the fourth grade. The CRCT may not be the sole determinor, however: Other factors such as attendance and performance on local assessment tests could also be considered.

> **Testing *en Español*—and Other Special Cases**
>
> The current criteria for whether children can take these tests in another language are quite tricky. The rules are complex enough to warrant a book of their own, but in the end it boils down to a decision by the local school board about whether a student has completed enough study in English to take the CRCT. As for students with disabilities, the state of Georgia has several different CRCT formats, such as Braille and audiotape. Parents should check with their local school districts to find out the CRCT options available.

How You Can Help

Many of you are already aware of how important state standardized tests are to your child, which is why you picked up this book in the first place. While the teacher is probably already doing some exam-related work in the classroom, nothing is better for your child than receiving personal tutoring from someone he trusts. Since Mr. Rogers is very busy this time of year, that person will have to be you. Contained inside this book are all the facts, tips, questions, activities, and advice you will need to help your child succeed on the CRCT. *Parent's Guide to the Georgia CRCT for Grade 3* lets you know exactly what skills are being tested on these exams, gives you test-taking strategies to make approaching these tests easier, and tells you exactly how to teach your child these skills and strategies. By analyzing and discussing the tests in detail, our goal is not only to provide you and your child with the basic knowledge he needs to excel on the tests, but also to instill a sense of confidence through familiarity, since feeling confident and prepared is a key factor in how a student fares on the tests.

After reading this book, both you and your child should feel ready to take on the tests first—and then the fourth grade. While that feeling might not do you any good in your adult life, it will do wonders for your kid.

Chapter One: THE A's, B's, C's, AND D's OF GOOD TEST TAKING

Does the mere sight of a No. 2 pencil cause your child to break into a cold, trembling sweat? Are the words *multiple-choice* or *standardized test* invariably followed by a thin, keening shriek or forlorn wail? If the answer to either of these questions is "yes," then it's time you faced the facts: When it comes to taking standardized tests, your child is just like everyone else.

The vast majority of Americans experience some fear and nervousness before taking a big test. It is only natural that a eight-year-old would feel anxious when faced with a test that might cause him to be held back a grade. Sure, there are a few folks out there who are perfectly calm when faced with exams, but they are all either hopelessly insane or currently making a living writing test-preparation materials.

The Breakdown

Each CRCT subject test is given in two different sessions of 45–60 minutes apiece.

Subject Test	No. of Questions
Mathematics	60 questions
English Language Arts	50 questions
Reading	40 questions

Note: The number of questions listed here indicate only those problems which count towards a student's score. Each CRCT also contains field-tests items that will not be included in your child's score. (We'll discuss these questions later in this chapter.)

As the Social Studies and Science CRCTs have yet to be implemented, we have few details about them, although it's a good bet that your third grader will see 50 or 60 questions, plus some field-test items, on each test.

Let your kid know that it is normal to be nervous about the unknown, but that the more he knows about the CRCT assessments, the less nervous he will feel. All the information and all the techniques we will cover in this book will ease your child's nervousness and replace it with confidence by making that "unknown"—in this case, the exams—familiar and manageable. Test anxiety almost invariably leads to a lower test score, so it is important that you work to boost your child's confidence about the exams. Just understanding the basic format of these exams can be empowering, as the Reading CRCT changes from a scary hurdle that must be jumped to simply "a multiple-choice test that will include some passages for me to read."

Learning about question types and other facts about the exams serves a dual purpose: It provides your child with useful information, and it takes away the fear-of-the-unknown aspect of the test. This principle is the foundation of successful test preparation:

Familiarity leads to confidence.

Think of the Georgia tests as that haunted house on the end of your street. At first, your child only knows the horror stories about the children who went inside never to be seen again. Your job as a parent is to guide your child through the exams during the day, showing how the scary noise coming from upstairs is caused by a rusty blind, and that beyond the usual dangers associated with an old house (loose floorboards, a rickety staircase), there is nothing about the place to worry about. If you can replace the anxiety and stress your child feels about the CRCT assessments with a feeling of confidence, you will have done him a great service.

Why Cosmas Ndeti, Former Boston Marathon Winner, Would Probably Do Well on the CRCT

Although Mr. Ndeti, a world-class marathon runner, probably has not had as much work with fractions as your child has recently, he is very skilled in one crucial test-taking area: *pacing*. Knowing that he's going to run 26 miles, Ndeti picks a nice, consistent speed at which to run, and keeps at that pace throughout the entire race. What he *doesn't* do, and what you should not allow your child to do, is spend too much time in any one area or run out of gas before the race is over.

The main idea you must pass on to your child now is not to spend too much time on any question. At a certain point, taking too much time becomes as harmful as taking too little: frustration mounts, boredom and fatigue set in. Perseverance is a noble trait, but on a standardized test, spending half the time answering one multiple-choice question is tantamount to standardized-test suicide. Your child should stay focused on the task at hand and never get too flustered by any one question.

One or two small breaks during each test is fine if your child feels her brain is getting strained. Tell her to put the pencil down, stretch out her hands and arms, think of eating her favorite food, and then pick up the pencil and finish the test. If your child comes to a question she does not understand, tell her to think of this as a guideline:

> ***Spend up to three minutes trying to figure out what the question is truly driving at; then, using the techniques taught in this book, take an educated guess and move on.***

The CRCT does not require perfection. There are only two real scores: pass or fail. To pass, students simply need to get about two thirds of the questions right, so it is never worth their while to spend 40 minutes on one question that's stumping them, only to be so mentally fatigued that they do poorly on the rest of the exam. Certainly, you don't want to encourage your child to do less than her best, but she must realize that no one question is so important that it is worth getting bogged down on and upset over. There are always some questions that just seem baffling. Throughout the rest of this book, we'll show you how to show your kid how to make good guesses, keep her cool, and stay on pace when faced with a stumper.

In addition to telling your child not to get stuck on one question, you can also encourage the "two-pass" approach to test taking. On the first pass through a test, your child should answer only those questions she can handle quickly and easily, skipping over any questions that leave her confused or require a lot of thought. Seeing a bunch of ovals filled in right away often gives students a quick boost of confidence. On the second pass, tell your child to go a little slower, use process of elimination (a technique we'll discuss in a moment) to cross out any incorrect choices, and then take a guess and move on. The two-pass system is very helpful on all of the CRCT exams, since it allows your child to answer the easy multiple-choice questions before tackling the more difficult ones.

To help illustrate the importance of pacing, you might want to share this little "test-prep fable" with your child.

KAPLAN'S TEST-PREP FABLES: THE TALE OF ISHMAEL THE SNAIL

Call him Ishmael the snail. When all the fish signed up for the annual aquarium obstacle-course race, no one gave him much of a chance, but Ishmael was confident of his abilities. The starting gun sounded, and all the contestants took off. The goldfish Ahab took the lead, but he got caught up on a whale of an obstacle early on. He couldn't figure out how to get around it, and he never finished the race. The two clown loaches were also very fast, but they made too many mistakes. They kept swimming under the hurdles instead of over them, and they skipped some obstacles completely, so they wound up being disqualified. The gourami started out at a good clip, but he fell fast asleep around the plastic plant and Ishmael passed him up. Ishmael ran the entire course at a steady, constant pace, rarely making mistakes, and when the final results were tallied, Ishmael was the winner. As his reward, Ishmael was named king of the aquarium. He now lives in a plastic castle and rules the other fish wisely and fairly.

Moral: A steady pace wins the race.

Edgar Allan P.O.E. for the CRCT

One of the biggest advantages to taking a multiple-choice test is that you don't always have to know the correct answer choice. Think about it: The answer is already there, staring you in the face. If you find all the incorrect answer choices and eliminate them, you will get the question right just the same. The *process of elimination* technique, known as P.O.E. in test taker's lingo, is one that good test takers use instinctively, but that anyone can learn to do with practice. It is especially helpful on the Georgia tests because there is no guessing penalty. You see, on some standardized tests, a fraction of a point is deducted from a student's final score for every question answered incorrectly. This is known as a *guessing penalty,* and it is meant to discourage random guessing. On the CRCT, no points are deducted. A wrong answer simply results in zero credit, not negative credit, so your child has nothing to lose and everything to gain by making good guesses on questions he is having trouble answering. And P.O.E. is the key to good guessing.

To demonstrate the effectiveness of this technique, see if your child can answer the following question.

1. How old are the authors of this book?
    A. 4 years old
    B. 29 years old
    C. 35 years old
    D. 126 years old

If this weren't a multiple-choice question, your child would have little to no chance of getting the question right. However, as it stands, he should have narrowed down the choices to either B or C, giving him a fifty-fifty shot of guessing correctly. Since, as we mentioned, there is no penalty for guessing, he should then pick either B or C and move on to the next question.

Use Process of Elimination to cross out incorrect answer choices.

Perhaps the hardest part about using P.O.E. is knowing when to use it. In the above question, for example, how would you know that A and D were incorrect? You could say you used common sense, and that would be a valid answer. In many ways common sense translates to a basic understanding of what the question is asking, and therefore what the possible answers could be. Ask your child the question below, and help him use common sense to get a general idea of what the answer will be.

> Thomas had $4.00, but he gave half of his money away to his friend Jeremy for a plastic bucket. Then Thomas gave away half of his remaining money to buy some gum. How much money does Thomas now have?

Before looking at the answer choices, ask your child the following questions:

> Could Thomas now have more than $4.00?
>
> Could Thomas have no money at all?
>
> Could Thomas have $2.00?

The answer to all these questions is *no*. The last question is probably the toughest. But even if that question is confusing to your child, he could still look at the answer choices and eliminate some incorrect responses.

THE A's, B's, C's, AND D's OF GOOD TEST TAKING

    A. $4.00
    B. $2.00
    C. $1.00
    D. $0.00

Why would answer choice A even be offered? Test designers put it there to catch the careless student. They know many students often glance at a question, feel unsure of how to work the problem, and just pick a number from the question that appears in the answer choices. Using the process of elimination—and thinking about what the question is really asking—can help your child avoid these mistakes.

Your child can also apply P.O.E. in the Reading CRCT. The incorrect choices are generated the same way they are in the above question: Words are taken from the reading passage and placed out of context as an answer choice. Students who remember seeing the words in the passage mistakenly pick them as an answer choice, never questioning whether the answer makes sense. Here's an adaptation of a recent question:

2. Where did Farmer Ike keep his cows?
    A. in the barn
    B. in a fenced-in pasture
    C. at a fruit stand
    D. in his house

Which of these choices can be eliminated? We hope your child will recognize C and D as unlikely correct answers. C is wrong because stacking cows into pyramids is much harder than stacking apples and oranges, and D is unlikely because no farmer likes to have dinner interrupted by a stampede crashing through the kitchen. Still, these were actual answer choices, because the words *fruit stand* and *house* appeared in the reading passage.

Have an Answer for Everything

Suppose your child comes to a multiple-choice math question that she can't figure out at all. She spends some time looking over the answer choices to see if there are any she feels she can cross out, but nothing comes to mind. Process of

> **The Number One and Only Child in the Class**
>
> Students are naturally leery of answering a question they do not feel they know the answer to, and they prefer not to say anything unless they are absolutely sure they are right. Teachers see this all the time in classrooms: Children refuse to raise their hands and offer answers to questions because they are afraid of being embarrassed by a wrong answer. Unfortunately, this habit will hurt your child's test score. So explain to your child that on these exams, she should act as if she is the only student in her favorite teacher's class, and if she does not answer, the teacher will just stand there until she does.

elimination fails her. Should she leave this question blank and move on to the next question? The answer is "No, no, no, no, no, a thousand times no!" Again, there is no guessing penalty on the CRCT subject tests, so every question must be filled in, even if it means random guessing instead of educated guessing (although educated guessing using P.O.E. is always better, of course). Advise your child to:

1. **Look for ways to work the problem using the appropriate skill.**

2. **Use P.O.E. to cross out incorrect answer choices.**

3. **Guess and move on, knowing that a test grade does not depend on every little question.**

If your child needs further convincing about the benefits of guessing, you might try telling the following story:

KAPLAN'S TEST-PREP FABLES: THE STORY OF KRONHORST THE FUZZY CHIHUAHUA BUNNY

Early in his life Kronhorst was just like all the other bunnies. He enjoyed carrots, frolicking in a pasture, and hopping up and down to his heart's content. One day, though, the Bunny Master came to all the bunnies in the world and said, "Okay, it's time you all got ears." (This happened a long time ago, when all bunnies were earless.) The bunnies had several choices to pick from: "long and floppy," "really long and floppy," and "tastefully long and floppy," just to name a few. Every bunny made a choice except Kronhorst, who couldn't pick between "cute and floppy" and "trippily floppy."

Not making a choice was the worst thing that ever happened to Kronhorst, because from that point on, everyone he met always mistook him for a fuzzy Chihuahua. "Look at that way too hairy Chihuahua!" people would cry, at which point Kronhorst would have to explain that he was a bunny. People would then ask, "But where are your ears?" Needless to say, Kronhorst got pretty tired of these conversations, as well as the endless invitations to the Hair Club's Annual Dog Show... although later in life he did make a lot of money investing in the stock market.

Moral: Answer every question on the exam or people will confuse you for a fuzzy Chihuahua.

The Only Way to Avoid Mental Mistakes

There is nothing gained by your child's trying to solve any of these problems in his head. While it is impressive if your child can multiply big numbers without using pencil and paper, or work out scientific experiments in his head, it's not required for the Georgia CRCT. In fact, it even works against his score. Get your child into the habit of writing down all his work on problems and jotting down the main idea of a reading passage as he goes through it. Kids can eliminate a slew of careless errors simply by writing down their work. For many children, writing things down helps them clarify the material. Writing down work during practice sessions also makes for a better learning experience: If your child misses a question, at least you can go back together and see what the problem was.

Write down all work whenever possible.

In some parts of the Math CRCT, all that your child needs to do to give himself a great shot at getting the right answer is remember to write down all his work neatly.

The Field-Test Questions

"Field-test questions" are the name the Georgia Department of Education (GDOE) has given to all items on the CRCT assessments that do not count towards a student's grade. Each subject test contains ten such questions, which means that 14–20 percent of each exam is comprised of field-test questions—in other words, as much as 20 percent of the questions your child faces will not count towards her final score.

These questions let the GDOE experiment with problems that could appear on future tests. So on one hand, the field-test items are helpful to future test takers because they allow the GDOE to determine if the new questions are too hard or too easy. But on the other hand, your child will have to take the time to answer a lot of questions that have no bearing on her test score. The presence of these questions just reinforces that it is never wise to get hung up on any one question: Your child might be exerting all her brainpower to solve a question that doesn't even count towards her score. Remind your child never to get flustered by any question.

"'Twas the Night Before the Test . . ."

Make sure your child feels confident and well rested on the days of the test. Hopefully, this means keeping the nightly routine as regular as possible. You might want to schedule some sort of activity for the nights during the tests, but it should *not* be cramming. Trying to jam in tons of information before a test session is not conducive to a child's test-taking confidence, and it should be avoided.

A positive attitude is more important than any one fact.

If your child does want to review for a while, stick to the basics, asking questions about the test format and general test-taking strategies. These will come in handier than reviewing any particular parts of the different tests. Also, your child will probably answer most of the general test format questions correctly, which will boost his confidence. What you do not want is to have your child stumped by a series of questions, because then he will go into the exam the next day thinking he is going to do badly.

PARENT'S GUIDE TO THE GEORGIA CRCT FOR GRADE 3

Here's a handy list of pointers for the time before the exam:

THINGS TO DO BEFORE THE EXAM

1. Make sure your child gets an adequate amount of rest.
2. Give your child a healthy breakfast.
3. Let your child have any medication if and only if he takes that medication on a regular basis.
4. Participate in some activity at night that is fun for your child but not too taxing. (Watching a movie on the VCR or playing board games are two ideas.)
5. Give your child positive words of encouragement right before he goes to take the test.

You get the main idea. Send your kid to school relaxed and positive, and don't do anything to upset his normal rhythm. Some things that would *definitely* upset his normal rhythm and as such should be avoided at all costs are included in the following list:

THINGS NOT TO DO BEFORE THE EXAM

1. Send him to bed earlier than usual, because he will just lie in bed thinking about the test.
2. Let your child have any noncritical medication (such as over-the-counter cold or allergy medicine) that will cause drowsiness or muddled thinking.
3. Decide to unwind by watching the midnight tripleheader of Scream I, II, and III.
4. Decide that the morning of the test is the perfect time to explain to your child how big the national debt really is, and what that will mean to him.

Review

The Main Points Your Child Should Know:

1. Understand the format of all the CRCT subject tests, and be comfortable with them.
2. Maintain a consistent pace throughout the test, and don't let any single question fluster you.
3. Use process of elimination whenever possible.
4. Answer every question.
5. Write down all work to avoid foolish mental mistakes.
6. Make sure you are relaxed and positive on test day.

Questions to Ask Your Child:

1. What's the moral of "Ishmael the Snail"? *A steady pace wins the race.*
2. Ask general questions about the test format until your child answers the queries easily. *How many multiple-choice questions are on the Reading CRCT? How many answer choices for every question?*
3. What does P.O.E. stand for? *Process of elimination.* Why would you want to use P.O.E.? *Because finding incorrect answers and crossing them out gives you a better chance of answering a question correctly.*
4. What's the moral of "Kronhorst the Fuzzy Chihuahua"? *Answer every question on the test or be mistaken for a Chihuahua with a hair problem.*
5. When you should solve questions in your head? *Never!*
6. Who will love you no matter how you do on these exams? *Your parents, of course!*

Chapter Two READING

Questions on the third-grade Reading CRCT follow reading passages that are usually about 400–1,000 words in length. The number of questions per passage varies, but correlates to the passage length (the longer a passage is, the more questions that follow). Some of the reading passages may be culled from existing sources, such as *Cricket* and *Jack and Jill* magazines, which contain amusing, educational, and generally positive stories. If you want to give your child more practice at reading material similar to what will appear on the Reading CRCT—thus lessening his fear of the unknown—then you should:

Go to a bookstore or library and start reading children's magazines with your child.

This will help on many levels. It will give your child more exposure to reading testlike passages, it should aid in his understanding of such passages (provided you help him with positive guidance), and it should improve your child's overall reading ability. And, as if that weren't enough, it's also quality time!

As for passage types, the selections tend more towards fiction than nonfiction, with folk tales being a popular genre. However, have your child prepared for a wide variety of formats, because rest assured, there will be some odd passage types.

In general, multiple-choice questions after a reading passage fall into four major categories:

    Word Meanings

    Supporting Ideas

    Summarization

    Generalizations and Inferences

Before we can start discussing each category, we will need a reference passage, such as the sample reading passage that follows.

Dashiell Learns a Lesson

There once was a young ant named Dashiell who loved to play all the time. Dashiell enjoyed spending time playing with his friends more than anything else in the world.

It was fall, and time for all the ants in the meadow to trek to their winter anthill in the forest. Most of the ants were busy moving their possessions, because they did not want to get caught in the meadow when the cold weather and snow came. Dashiell started to move some of his items, but then the weather was so nice that he decided to take a break and enjoy the sun for a while.

Boing, boing! sounded through the meadow. Dashiell watched as Rebecca Rabbit hopped up next to him.

"Where are you going?" asked Dashiell.

"I'm enjoying the day by hopping back and forth across the meadow. It's very fun, would you like to join me?" asked Rebecca.

"Hopping seems like a lot of fun," thought Dashiell. He raised up his hind legs and tried jumping like Rebecca did, but soon fell over on his face. When he looked up he saw that Aunt Dawn had crawled up beside him.

"You still need to move your possessions to the winter anthill," said Aunt Dawn. "There's no better time than the present." Then Aunt Dawn crawled away towards the winter anthill.

Dashiell was about to go back to work, but then he saw Sylvester Snake pass nearby. "That looks like a fun way to travel," he thought. Dashiell laid his body on the ground and tried to slither like the snake did. He twisted his body on the ground for some time, but never made any progress. He stopped once his stomach started to get sore. Aunt Dawn saw Dashiell on her way back to her anthill and said, "All your belongings still need to be moved from the summer house. There's no better time than the present."

"Aunt Dawn is right, I should stop playing." Dashiell walked through the meadow. He heard the flutter of wings above his head. Dashiell looked up to see Carol Crow flying around in the air above him.

"What are you doing?" asked Dashiell.

"I'm flying around in search of food," replied Carol Crow, who snatched a tasty grasshopper out of the air.

"Flying seems like fun. Will you help me try to fly?" said Dashiell. He climbed up a nearby rock until he reached the top. Then he jumped off while waving his legs. Dashiell fell to the ground on his face. "Yipes," he cried, rubbing his head. Dashiell looked up and saw Aunt Dawn standing beside him.

"You still need to move all your belongings. There's no better time than the present." Aunt Dawn left to get more of her possessions and shook her head. "Will Dashiell ever figure it out?" she wondered.

READING

As the sun set that day Dashiell finally got tired of playing. "Time to get to work," he said. He went to the summer anthill and picked up some of his possessions. Just then a huge rainstorm broke out. Dashiell was unable to leave the summer anthill, and had to spend the night in the cold, wet anthill all by himself.

The next morning at the winter anthill, Aunt Dawn awoke and saw Dashiell crawling inside with a load of his clothing. "I thought you were going play all day again," said Aunt Dawn.

Dashiell placed the pieces of clothing down and replied, "I need to move all my belongings here. There's no better time than the present."

Aunt Dawn laughed. "I'm glad you learned that lesson, Dashiell. Put that clothing away, and then let's go get more of your possessions to move to our winter anthill."

Dashiell Learned His Lesson: Now It's Your Child's Turn

While reading through this passage, your child should be thinking about finding the main idea. What is the whole story about? Having a main idea helps shape the entire story, giving it meaning, which hopefully should help your child in her understanding. However, while learning the main idea is important, *memorizing* it is not something your child needs to do. The passage is not going anywhere after your child reads it. It stays right there for easy reference. Teach her to:

Read to understand, not to memorize.

Once your child understands the action of the story, it's time to start answering the questions. Kids sometimes try to read the story and then answer the questions without looking back into the passage for help. If she does this, events could get jumbled together, which will only lead to incorrect answer choices. Tell your child that the Reading CRCT is just like an open-book test. The passage is there for her to refer to, so teach her to feel comfortable going back to the passage to help her answer questions correctly.

Looking For Main Ideas Everywhere

If your child is unclear on what finding the main idea means, ask him simply to tell you a story about something that happened to him at school that day. Since almost every story should have a point, when your child finishes his story, ask him to name the most important thing about what he just said. Another way to phrase this is "If you had to retell the point of the story again in only one sentence, what would that sentence be?" The most important thing should be the main idea.

Looking at a newspaper and discussing how headlines capture the main idea of a news story is another way to talk about the main idea. You can then read the story and come up with your own headlines. One exception: Stay away from articles dealing with intricate, high-level finance, unless you want your child's head to explode. By the way, if your child likes headlines, you can always play "Night of the Headlines!" where one night everyone speaks only in catchy, single sentences, such as "Child Heads for Bathroom!" or "Argument over TV Remote Leads to Conflict, Then Grounding."

Word Meanings

Some of the tougher words (or phrases) in the passage will have questions devoted to them, asking your child "What does _____ mean?" It is then up to your child to figure out the meaning of the word by looking at the context, or how the word is used in the passage. Reading or hearing words in context is actually a good way for children to learn new vocabulary. It should be stressed that these are supposed to be new words, so your child should not be bothered if the word is foreign to him.

To help your child sharpen his ability to understand words in context, have him focus on the meaning of the entire sentence in which the word appears. Remember, in a multiple-choice item the answer is already there, so your child just needs a pretty good idea of what the italicized word in the question might mean in order to tell which answer choice is correct. Sometimes the meaning of the unknown word can be gleaned from the sentence it is in, but if the meaning is not there, then either the sentence before or the sentence after will contain the necessary context clues. Your child should never have to look any further than that—this is a third-grade test, after all. As he looks over these sentences, have him circle any clue words that he feels help him understand the meaning of the word. In other words,

Read above and below the unknown word.

After he does this, he should be able to answer a question like this one:

1. In the story, Dashiell thinks it would be fun to slither like Sylvester Snake. What does *slither* mean?
   A. slide
   B. fly
   C. hop
   D. crawl

Hopefully, your child chose answer choice A, "slide." As you can see, Word Meanings questions do not ask students to give the exact dictionary definition of *slither*, just to choose the word or phrase that is synonymous with its meaning. When you ask your kid which words led him to that answer, he should say the words "like the snake did" and the phrase "twisted his body on the ground."

If your child prefers, tell him to look over the questions before reading each passage, and see if there are any Word Meanings questions for that passage. If there are, your child

---

THE MACKINUTE GAME

A fun way to help your child learn about context is to play the Mackinute Game. Take turns with your child substituting the word *mackinute* into a regular sentence. The other player has to guess what the word *mackinute* means in that sentence. For instance, you might say, "I like my hamburgers with pickles, lettuce, tomato, and plenty of mackinute." If your child answers "ketchup" or "mustard" or some other likely answer, ask her to pick out the words that helped her figure out the definition of the word. Try to make the game as silly as possible. Good luck, and may the best person mackinute!

should pay close attention to the unknown word in question when he reads the passage, in the hopes of understanding its meaning right away. This may help him feel more empowered about the test, but if it makes him lose track of the overall storyline, it's not worth doing. In that case, just have him read the entire story and then be prepared to go back to where the word is in the passage.

Let's try another question:

2. Dashiell raises up on his hind legs in the story. What does *hind* mean?
    A. rear
    B. above
    C. top
    D. front

> **THE MACKINUTE GAME, VERSION 2**
>
> In this variation of the Mackinute Game, the rules are the same as before, but the person now has to identify which words acted as clues in the sentence. So, when Player 1 says, "I left the mackinute in the oven too long and burnt its crust," Player 2 now has to say which words (*oven*, *crust*) led him to guess that the mackinute was a "pie."

The sentence with the word *hind* in it contains clues like "raised up on" and "fell over on his face," which might be enough for your child to figure out that *hind* must mean "back" or "rear." However, the sentence before also contains a clue, since Dashiell is discussing "hopping," an activity that every creature on the planet, whatever it might be, usually does with its back limbs.

Supporting Ideas

Plainly speaking, "supporting ideas" questions test how well students have read and understood small pieces of the passage. These questions are not about the "main idea." They are about the little details that, combined, make up the whole of the passage. For example, say you told your child the following story:

> A clown in a blue suit walks into a bank with a large duck on his head. The clown goes up to a teller, who asks, "Is it hard to keep that thing balanced like that?"
>
> "Not really," replied the duck. "I've got sticky webbed feet."

The Supporting Ideas questions would be things like "What color suit was the clown wearing?" or "What size was the duck?" These questions ask your child small facts about the passage that she is not likely to remember. If she tries to approach this Reading test the way she takes most tests (i.e., by answering questions from memory to test her knowledge), these Supporting Ideas queries are going to trip her up. Therefore, when looking at the Reading test booklet, it is important for your child to keep in mind that:

The answers for all Supporting Ideas questions are waiting for you in the passage.

PARENT'S GUIDE TO THE GEORGIA CRCT FOR GRADE 3

This is another way of saying be sure to look in the passage to answer Supporting Ideas questions. Your child need not trust her memory on the Reading CRCT. Remind her that this is an "open book" test, and using the passage is the best way to get these questions right. From memory, can either you or your child remember which animal Dashiell plays with first? Even if you think you can, it is smart to refer to the passage to answer this question:

3. Which is the first animal that Dashiell plays with?
   A. Carol Crow
   B. Aunt Dawn
   C. Rebecca Rabbit
   D. Sylvester Snake

Looking back into the passage, your child should be able to choose C or to eliminate A, B, and D, leaving C to pick. Either way, it's the correct response.

Here is another question:

4. Which animal in the story says, "There's no better time than the present"?
   A. Carol Crow
   B. Aunt Dawn
   C. Rebecca Rabbit
   D. Dashiell

If your child decides not to look back at the passage, she might carelessly pick D. And she would be wrong! A review of the passage would lead her to the correct response, B.

Knowing where to look takes some understanding of the passage, but with practice your child should get better at reading a passage for its main idea while keeping a general idea of what events occurred when. Then answering Supporting Ideas questions becomes simply a matter of heading to a particular paragraph, reviewing the information, and answering correctly.

Summarization

There will undoubtedly be multiple-choice questions that ask, "Hey, what's the big idea?" More specifically, these questions want to know, "Hey, what's the main idea of this particular story?" Your child can learn to recognize these questions fairly easily, as the majority of them are usually written using phrases like: "This story is mostly about ____," "What's the main idea of this story?" and "Which sentence best tells about this story?"

Recognizing what kind of question is being asked is very important, since the question type determines the strategies your child should use to answer it. In this case, knowing

READING

that a particular question is a Summarization question is vital, since it means that the answer is *not* stated specifically in the passage. Your child could reread the passage forever and still not find the answer. That's why you should explain that . . .

 To answer the "mostly about" questions, get the Big Picture.

Your child will have to glean a general idea of what the reading passage is about, and then use process of elimination when reviewing the answer choices. Having a general idea of the meaning of the passage helps students separate the right answer from the wrong ones, which is another reason why working on finding the main idea with your child is such a useful activity. The wrong choices are often actual facts from the passage, so they can be very appealing options. But remind your child that just because a piece of information appears in the passage doesn't make it the *main* idea. A good way to think about it—and if your child can understand this, he's on his way to a successful career as a standardized test taker—is that wrong answers on Summarization questions are often the right answer on Supporting Ideas questions, and vice versa. Get it?

Have your child think about the Dashiell passage, and what the point of the story was, and then attempt the following question:

> **How Watching TV Can Help Improve Your Child's Score**
>
> Granted, there's a catch: It has to be educational television. But if your child enjoys watching nature shows, one way to practice Summarization is to ask him to summarize sections of these shows in his own words. Nature shows, on channels ranging from Discovery to PBS, are almost always broken down into segments like "Here's how the meercats defend their territory" or "Two rams fight to see who's the toughest ram in the herd" or "Here a pack of hyenas go to the automated teller machine to get some money for the baseball doubleheader." This game can be played with other shows, but nature shows are a good place to start. This is because nature segments often have a general point, yet one that is never stated outright by the narrator who is often spending all his time trying to sound majestic.

5. What is this story mostly about?

   A. Dashiell tried other ways of moving but learned that the ant way works the best for him.

   B. A rabbit, a snake, and a crow all showed Dashiell how they move around the meadow.

   C. Dashiell carried food from the meadow to the anthill and back again.

   D. A crow flew by Dashiell, caught a grasshopper, and then flew away.

17

While B, C, and D are all factual, none of them encapsulates the main point of the story, which is A.

Generalizations and Inferences

Inference questions, as you might expect, compel the student to infer an answer not stated specifically in the passage. Sometimes the question will have a phrase like *will most likely* in it, showing that the answer is not 100 percent definite, only very likely. Like Summarization questions, Inference questions force the student to understand the passage and make deductions from it. For example, after the passage:

> Sheryl was sick, but her brother Tommy, who was in grade school, felt fine. Sheryl's three best friends in high school were Angela, Tammy, and Brenda. Brenda lived next door, while Angela and Tammy lived across town.

An Inference question would be:

> Since Sheryl is sick, who will probably to take her homework to school for her?
> A. Tommy
> B. Angela
> C. Tammy
> D. Brenda

While this example may seem a little arbitrary (What if Tommy's grade school was next door to Sheryl's high school? What if Brenda went to a private school?), the question does contains the phrase *will probably*, which goes to show you that the GDOE (Georgia Department of Education) knows the meaning of CYA.

From the Dashiell passage, a Generalizations and Inferences question might look like:

6. In the passage, Aunt Dawn kept telling Dashiell "there's no better time than the present" over and over again because she —
    A. wanted him to forget his chores and play all the time
    B. wanted him to stop delaying the important work he needed to do
    C. needed help moving her belongings
    D. wanted him to be the first ant to move into the winter anthill

Nowhere in the passage does it explicitly state Aunt Dawn's reason for constantly telling Dashiell, "There's no better time than the present." It is up to your child to deduce from the passage that Aunt Dawn tells Dashiell this because she "wanted him to stop delaying the important work he needed to do"—answer B.

Process of Elimination can also be used on question 6. It is important for your child to realize that these passages are written at the third-grade level, and when it comes to emotions:

Good feelings beat bad feelings most of the time.

The reading passages are not written by a bitter, impoverished author angry at the world, no matter what anyone else tells you. They are written by former educators, and because of this there are no depressing stories about gambling addiction or people fighting and dying in a senseless war. So if there is an Inference question that asks how a teacher feels, answer choices like "angry," "hateful," or "moronic" can always be crossed out, and if a question asks why an aunt is acting a certain way towards her nephew, surely the reasons are going to be positive ones. Aunt Dawn, then, is not going to believe choice A, which is negative, or at least not very parental of her. The best answer choice is B, as it is just the sort of positive, character-building answer that former educators writing the test would want children to learn.

Inference questions require your child to make some mental leaps, something that she may not be too willing to do. If your child is not so thrilled about trusting her own thoughts, here's a story to boost her confidence.

KAPLAN'S TEST-PREP FABLES: THE PRINCESS WHO WANTED TWO BADGERS AND CEMENT BOOTS

Everyone agreed that Princess Lori was without doubt the most beautiful and difficult person in the entire kingdom. When the king asked whose hand she wanted in marriage, Lori replied she would take the first man who came through the front castle door wearing cement boots and carrying a badger in each hand. From anyone else, this statement would have been called ridiculous, but coming from Lori it was not even the fourth most difficult request she made that day.

Lured by her beauty, many suitors tried, but all failed. These men learned the hard way that knocking on a door or turning a handle when carrying a badger is an almost impossible task, especially if you have sensitive fingers. And these men were better than most, who got shin splints from wearing cement shoes and never even made it out of the construction area.

But one day Umbagog the Woodsman came to the castle. A fierce man, Umbagog was so tough he normally cut down trees just by staring at them until they fell over in fright. Umbagog showed up outside the castle wearing cement shoes with steel girder laces while holding two of the biggest, meanest badgers anyone had ever seen. He took one look at the door, and then slammed his head against it, shattering it in one blow. Umbagog then married Princess Lori, and they both lived happily ever after for reasons no one could ever quite explain.

Moral: In tough situations, don't be afraid to use your head.

Another general point your child must remember is that pacing continues to be important throughout the Reading CRCT. Students sometimes spend way too long reading the passage, and then have no time to answer all the multiple-choice questions. Don't let this happen to your child. Tell her to:

Set a pace and watch your watch.

Of course, this means you will need to give your child a watch to wear (or make sure there is a clock in her classroom) and be certain sure she knows how to read it. Refer to the chart below for pacing suggestions:

> ### What Kind of Question is *That*?
>
> Knowing the differences between the four question categories helps you figure out how to approach each question. To work with your child and help him distinguish all categories, discuss the difference between the Word Meanings and Supporting Ideas categories, which require specific information from the passage, and the Summarization and Inference categories, which ask your child to interpret information from the passage.

Question	Time Spent
Reading the passage	2–5 minutes/passage
Multiple-choice questions	1–2 minutes/question

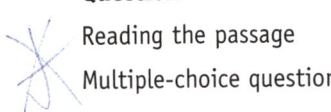

Once again, though, the key is not to spend too much on any one question at the expense of the entire test.

Chapter Three MATHEMATICS

The Grade 3 Mathematics CRCT consists of 60 multiple-choice questions (plus the ten field-test problems) that come from the following content areas:

1. Number Sense and Numeration
2. Geometry and Measurement
3. Patterns and Relationships/Algebra
4. Statistics and Probability
5. Computation and Estimation
6. Problem Solving

The rest of this chapter will discuss these various domains and provide you with techniques to help your child get better at these questions. Before we get started, though, here's a good rule of thumb on pacing during the Math CRCT: Take two minutes per question. Some students might take more time, others a little less. But if your child sticks to that schedule, he should be able to make one pass through the test answering all the easier questions, take a second pass for the harder problems, and then spend the rest of his time making any guesses necessary to answer every problem.

In general, obliquely worded questions create a good deal of confusion for Math CRCT takers. Questions in this section are rarely as straightforward as "Divide 48 by 6"; instead, the questions are often trying to see not whether students can divide, but if they know *when* the right time to divide is. To accomplish this, the question "Divide 48 by 6" might appear as:

> There are 48 people who need to be seated at 6 different tables. Each table must have the same number of people seated there. How many people will be seated at each table?
>
> A. 6
> B. 8
> C. 24
> D. 48

PARENT'S GUIDE TO THE GEORGIA CRCT FOR GRADE 3

Or the same question might be seen as this:

> There are 48 people who need to be seated at 6 different tables. Each table must have the same number of people seated there. How many people will be seated at each table?
>
> A. 48 ÷ 6 =
> B. 48 ÷ 8 =
> C. 48 × 6 =
> D. 48 × 8 =

All three of these questions pose the same math problem, but to answer the second and third questions correctly, the student must figure out that "hey, this is a division question." In essence, this approach is prevalent throughout the CRCT, which is why many intelligent kids get frustrated and wind up with a low score. They know a certain math skill quite well, but they don't realize that the exam is often more interested in discerning if the students know when they're supposed to use that particular math skill. Once your child gets comfortable with this approach, the math section gets a little easier.

Having said that, let's jump right in, shall we?

Number Sense and Numeration

These questions test a student's knowledge and understanding of such basic math principles as whole numbers, integers, even/odd numbers, decimals, fractions, ratios, and percents (you know, all the basics you learned as a child but have long since forgotten). What makes these concepts difficult is how they are presented on the test. Some of the questions will be very straightforward, like this one:

70 quarters   15 quarters   33 quarters   25 quarters

1. Which of these piggy banks has an even number of quarters?
    A. 70 quarters
    B. 15 quarters
    C. 33 quarters
    D. 25 quarters

Unless your child makes a careless error, chances are good she will come up with choice A as the answer. Other problems, however, are not so obvious, such as this one:

MATHEMATICS

The students at Piedmont Elementary are collecting sticks for an art project. The pictures below show the number of sticks they have collected so far.

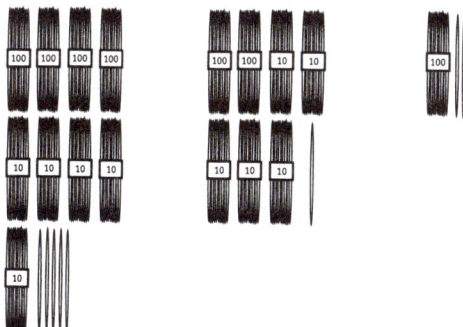

2. How many sticks do the students have after collecting them for three weeks?
    A. 808
    B. 880
    C. 708
    D. 826

This is a question that covers up what it is asking fairly well. The trick is for your child to not get flustered if she does not understand what to do initially. She should ask herself, "What does this question want me to do with all these numbers?" After some calm thought, she will probably realize the answer is "Add them together." If your child is able to get over any initial weirdness associated with this question, she should arrive at 808 (choice A) as her answer.

✓ Make sure your child is comfortable with basic math terms.

Some of the more popular terms to know are *fractions, ratios,* and *percents*. Your child can be fairly certain there will be a question or two on each of these topics, so it is important that she truly understands and feels comfortable with these subjects.

A question involving these terms might look like this:

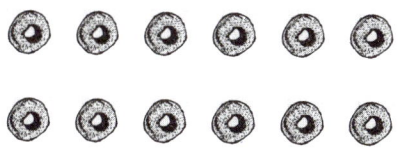

3. Evelyn has twelve doughnuts. 1/4 are glazed, 1/3 are chocolate, and the rest are plain. What fraction of the doughnuts are plain?

23

PARENT'S GUIDE TO THE GEORGIA CRCT FOR GRADE 3

A. 1/4
B. 1/3
C. 5/12
D. 7/12

On a question like the one above, just being able to recognize a fraction will not be enough to get it correct. Your child needs to have a clear understanding of how fractions work. In question 3, three of the doughnuts are glazed (1/4 of 12), and four are chocolate (1/3 of 12), leaving five doughnuts which must be plain. The answer would then be 5/12, choice C. Your child could have used P.O.E. to eliminate choices A and B, since both fractions appeared in the question itself.

> ### THE BRIBERY GAME
> One way to help your child work with fractions and other basic math terms is to play the Bribery Game. Assemble a collection of coins and then present various amounts of money to her and ask her how much she has. For percents, you should start with a dollar, since 100 cents = 1 dollar, so the number of cents is always the percentage of a dollar (25 cents = 25%). Gather like groups of currency together to work on fractions. For example, you might show your child a group of eight dimes and ask her, "If I had one fourth of these dimes, how many cents would I have?" For ratios, using two different groups of change would work. Present, say, six dimes and two nickels and ask, "What is the ratio of dimes to nickels?"

Geometry and Measurement

Geometry questions on the CRCT test students in several different categories.

Category	Example
Knowledge of different geometric shapes	How is a cylinder different from a cone?
Knowledge of geometric terms	What is symmetry? What is congruence?
Understanding of how an object will look if moved	What will Figure X look like if it it flipped upside down?

To tackle Geometry questions, your child will need to:

Know all the basic two- and three-dimensional figures.

Two-Dimensional	Three-Dimensional
Triangle	Pyramid (with triangular or rectangular base)
Square	Cube
Circle	Sphere
Rectangle	Cylinder
	Cone

MATHEMATICS

Knowing these figures is the critical first step to answering Geometry questions well. Knowing these definitions backward and forward is even better. Here is an example:

4. Which of the figures shown below is a rectangle?

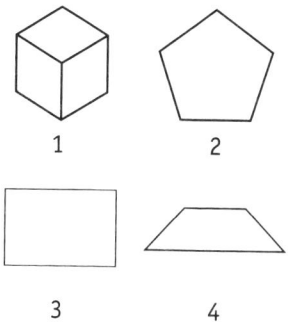

A. 1
B. 2
C. 3
D. 4

> ### SUGAR CUBE CASTLE
>
> For a fun way to teach your child about two- and three-dimensional shapes, buy a box or two of sugar cubes, get some glue, and construct a small castle using the cubes. All the basic shapes should be used: the towers could be cylinders, the front wall could be a rectangle composed of cubes, and pyramids and triangles could be placed along the tower wall. You may have to do some careful nibbling to make a sphere, but who doesn't like sugar?

If your child is knows his shapes, the answer, C, is fairly simple. If he doesn't know his shapes, then it's back to the sugar cubes for ye!

In addition to shapes, Geometry questions ask about such geometric terms as *congruence, symmetry, similarity,* and *reflections*. Again, though, questions on the Math CRCT will generally not be as straightforward as "What is the definition of congruency?" Instead, the question would give a figure, such as a rectangle, and then ask, "Which of the figures below is congruent to rectangle *ABCD*?" The student would then have to pick a congruent rectangle from among the answer choices. The correct answer will probably be "disguised" in some way, like being rotated 90 degrees.

Another type of Geometry question places an emphasis on spatial sense. Students get a nice, geometrical figure to start with, like this one:

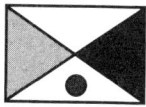

and are then asked to pick this figure out of a lineup after it has been spun, turned, or rotated in some way. For example:

25

PARENT'S GUIDE TO THE GEORGIA CRCT FOR GRADE 3

5. Which of the figures below shows the original figure after it has been flipped both vertically and horizontally?

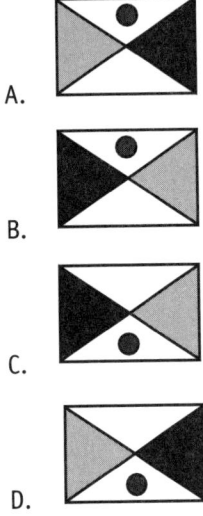

A.

B.

C.

D.

Two basic test-taking techniques come into play on a question like this. First, there is P.O.E., allowing your child to at least eliminate figure D, since it is the original figure. The second important strategy is "show your work." Do not have your child doing these mental flips in his head—have him draw the figure flipped horizontally and have him flip the figure vertically. Artistic brilliance is not necessary, and neither is an ability to figure out this question in his head. Your child should just sketch out the two flips, which should not take too long. Even if it does take four minutes, four minutes spent getting a question right is better than spending two minutes getting a question wrong. The answer is B.

Measurement questions on the Math CRCT test your child's knowledge of such measurements as length, width, area, volume, time, temperature, and angles. Questions in this content area might like look this:

6. Which is the most likely temperature for someone who is snowboarding?
    A. 100° F
    B. 72° F
    C. −72° F
    D. 27° F

All that is required is that your child understand the Fahrenheit scale. (Unless you are a polar bear, the answer is D.) Other questions involve reading a clock, so make sure your child is up on that.

MATHEMATICS

Another kind of Measurement problem centers around questions like, "Does your dog weigh 15 kilograms or 15 meters?" These Measurement problems test whether your child understands the basic units of measurement, and since no one uses metric units but everyone knows they should, you can expect that these problems will usually test metric terms. Here's an example:

7. Jimmy the Wonder Slug, shown below, was found recently on a South Pacific island. The picture shows the actual size of the slug. Which of the answer choices best describes the length of the slug?

   A. 5 kilometers
   B. 5 meters
   C. 5 centimeters
   D. 5 millimeters

If your child picks A, then she has probably had nightmares of monstrous slugs destroying whole cities in their slime trail. The correct unit of measurement is C, centimeters.

Patterns and Relationships/Algebra

"Prepare for launch: 6, 5, 4, 3, 2 . . . "

What number comes next? If your child knows the answer to that question, she is on the path to tackling Patterns questions. These questions often fall into one of two categories: "Find the Pattern" and "Add Up the Parts That Make Up the Pattern." A question that requires your child to find the pattern may look like this:

Study the pattern below.

8. What is the next shape in the pattern?

27

PARENT'S GUIDE TO THE GEORGIA CRCT FOR GRADE 3

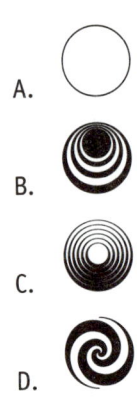

A. ◯

B. ◉

C. ◉

D. ◎

On questions like these, tell your child to be prepared for patterns in groups of four, like the problem above. Why? While it would be rash to say that there will always be four shapes that repeat, consider what the test designers' thought process must have been. They probably thought a pattern involving groups of two or three would be too easy. Five is a remote possibility, but six would be very difficult, so four it is! Since it is a four-character pattern above, the answer is A.

> ✶ **On questions involving repeating patterns, first look for patterns that repeat after every four characters.**

Questions which ask the student to add up the parts that make up the pattern are a little tougher, and they often look like the following problem:

This staircase is 4 steps high.

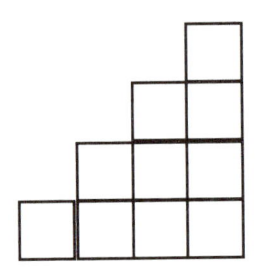

9. What would be the total number of squares if the staircase were 6 steps high?

    A. 10

    B. 15

    C. 21

    D. 24

28

MATHEMATICS

To solve this type of pattern problem, your child should *just continue the pattern and then add things up*. There are 10 squares to start with, so adding 5 squares and then 6 more would make 10 + 5 + 6 = 21 (C). Then it's off to the answer choices! Our old friend Process of Elimination could help if your child got stumped on this Pattern question. Clearly, if we started with 10 squares and then added more steps, choice A could not be correct. Your child can cross out this choice and then take a guess.

The Algebra portion of this content area contains many different-looking questions, since Algebra problems can be posed in many ways. However, many of them are similar to Pattern questions, and figuring out the pattern—and using some common sense—is all that is needed. Here's an example:

10. In the equation 4 + 7 + 3 = 7 + x + 4, what is the value of x ?
    A. 3
    B. 4
    C. 7
    D. 14

Variables such as x are a clear sign that this is an Algebra question, but this problem can be solved by using common sense. Your child should look at both sides of the equation: They're similar, aren't they, although the left side has a 3 whereas the right side has the variable x. Since both sides are equal, what's the best choice for x ? The correct answer is A. Your child could also get this problem correct simply by using P.O.E. and substituting each answer choice for x until she found the number that works.

Statistics and Probability

These questions normally involve graphs and charts. Simple graph problems may feature multiple questions referring to the same graph, and they look like this:

This graph shows how many raffle tickets Ms. Diaz's class sold during one week. Study the graph, then answer the questions that follow.

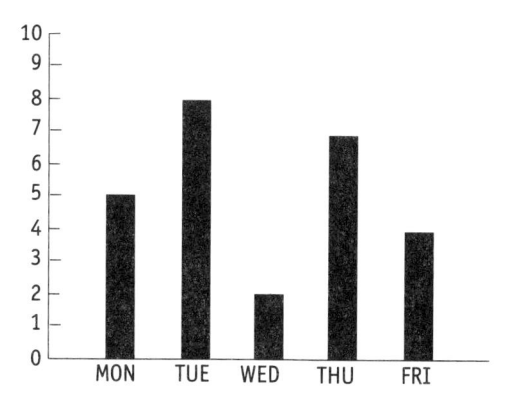

Ms. Diaz promised the class could work on their art project on the day the total number of tickets sold reached 16. The bar graph shows the number of tickets sold each day.

11. What day did Ms. Diaz let the class work on their art project?
    A. Friday
    B. Thursday
    C. Wednesday
    D. Tuesday

12. How many days did the students sell more than 6 tickets?
    A. 2
    B. 3
    C. 3
    D. 5

Neither question just asks for information from the chart, like "How many tickets were sold on Tuesday?" In each case, your child needs to read the graph and then use the information in some manner. In question 11, this means adding up the ticket sales each day until the number 16 is reached, on Thursday (B). Question 12 is essentially a P.O.E. question: Which days can be eliminated because fewer than 6 tickets were sold? Only two days are left—answer A.

In addition to charts and graphs, questions in this content domain will have some questions dealing with that other word, *Probability*. These questions can come in many different forms, so there is not really any one particular question setup your child should be on the lookout for. Luckily, there will probably not be very many of these questions on the exam. Don't spend too much time trying to explain the concept to your child. You may frustrate and worry him unnecessarily. If he is curious, you can try using a die to explain the general principle. Show him that there are six total sides on the die, each with a different number

> **FOR THOSE OF YOU SCORING AT HOME . . .**
>
> Various kinds of charts are scattered throughout every newspaper, but if you want to go to the place that charts call home, turn to the scoreboard page of the sports section. There you will always find as many charts as there were games last night. Explain to your child what the various markings mean, and then ask questions like "Who had the most hits in this baseball game?" or "How many more runs did the Braves score in the fourth inning than the Mets?" Questions like "This shortstop went hitless and yet still got paid $400,000 for the game. Where's the justice in that?" are socially relevant, but should not be asked to your child because they very rarely appear on the Math CRCT.

of dots. The probability that any side will appear when you roll the die is one in six. That's the basic idea. It is probably best to leave the discussion at that, unless you want to confuse yourself and your kid.

Computation and Estimation

Computation questions are pretty straightforward: They test your child on such mathematical basics as arithmetic properties, number sentences, and operations. Estimate questions are easy to spot because either they have the word *estimate* or the word *about* in them. At this point, your child should turn off her internal calculator and in its place put on her "I reckon" cap. Then she should:

Round off the numbers in the question, and then look at the answer choices.

Estimating questions are unusual because normally math tests prefer a precise answer as opposed to a ballpark figure. However, estimating is a useful skill to have—especially on later standardized tests such as the dreaded SAT. Let's look at the following problem:

13. The Fitzpatrick family drove 274 miles from Savannah to Marietta. Then they drove 104 miles from Marietta to Macon. About how many miles did they drive in all?
    - A. 200 miles
    - B. 300 miles
    - C. 400 miles
    - D. 500 miles

If your child rounded 274 to 300, and 104 to 100, the answer C becomes the only choice. And *I reckon* it's the right one.

Problem Solving

This is a bit of a catch-all category, where nonroutine problems have found a home. Here's an example of the type of question your child might see:

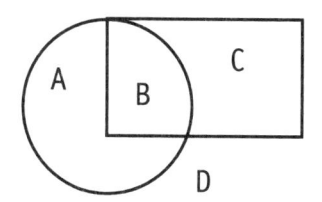

PARENT'S GUIDE TO THE GEORGIA CRCT FOR GRADE 3

14. Which letter is inside the circle and outside the rectangle?
    A. A
    B. B
    C. C
    D. D

If your child does not hurry through this question and make a careless mistake, and if he knows the definitions of a circle and a rectangle well enough not to somehow confuse the two shapes, then it should be no problem reaching A as the correct answer.

Whew! Believe it or not, that's all the math. It may seem like there is a lot for your child to remember. There is. But practice using the activities suggested in this chapter (and any others you can think of) and he will be up to speed in no time.

Chapter Four ENGLISH/ LANGUAGE ARTS

The English/Language Arts (ELA) CRCT contains 50 multiple-choice questions divided into the following four content areas:

- Grammar and Mechanics
- Paragraph Content and Organization
- Sentence Construction and Revision
- Research Process/Source Materials

With the exception of the last category, all of the questions in this portion of the CRCT deal with grammar. Now, normally hearing "grammar" sends children (and parents) running for the bomb shelter in an attempt to escape this hideous word. The aversion to grammar is generally caused by the fact that most people think they're very bad at it. While this is probably somewhat true, the fact is that most people are much better at grammar than they give themselves credit for.

Even though your everyday speech might not exemplify perfect grammar, that doesn't mean you can't recognize bad grammar from good grammar.

Since the ELA CRCT is all multiple-choice, all your child really has to concentrate on doing is to separate the correct answer choice from the incorrect ones. The strategies in this chapter will help make this task a much easier one to accomplish.

Grammar and Mechanics

Grammar questions often provide a piece of text, and then ask the student to locate and correct any errors in capitalization, punctuation, or spelling. Fortunately, the question itself will generally state which

Correct Check

Before tackling any question, your child should look at the answer choices to make sure there isn't a choice that says something like "correct as is." If there is, your child's goal is no longer to spot the error; first he must decide if there is a mistake or not. If he believes there's no error, he should pick "correct as is" and move on.

It's hard to say how many—if any—"correct as is" questions on the version of the ELA CRCT your child takes. Still, knowing about the possibility ahead of time will make your child better prepared for the exam.

33

PARENT'S GUIDE TO THE GEORGIA CRCT FOR GRADE 3

kind of error the student should be looking for. Have your child practice with the following examples of Grammar and Mechanics questions:

1. A comma is needed in the sentence below. Where should it be placed?

   We wanted to bring food, camping equipment and water on our journey into the mountains.

   A. after *camping*

   B. after *water*

   C. after *equipment*

   D. after *journey*

2. How can you correct the capitalization in the sentence below?

   We sent the package to governor Wilson, hoping he would appreciate our gift.

   A. put a capital *G* in *governor*

   B. put a capital *H* in *hoping*

   C. put a capital *P* in *package*

   D. Correct as is

3. The following sentence contains a spelling error. Pick the answer choice of the word not spelled correctly.

   Eager to get inside, Stan smashd his head into the screen door.

   A. Eager

   B. inside

   C. smashd

   D. screen

The two-pass system is the best way to approach the ELA CRCT. If your child is like most students, he is more comfortable spotting spelling errors than punctuation errors, so he would surely (shurely) benefit from answering these simpler questions before tackling harder ones. With this in mind, let's look at question 3 first. *Smashd* should be spelled *smashed*—improper suffixes and prefixes are always favorite spelling mistakes.

Eliminate What's Correct

If your child doesn't recognize *smashd* right away, there's always P.O.E. Have her cross out any choice that she is certain contains no spelling errors, and then take a guess. This won't work every time, but it's still a good way to garner extra points.

34

As for question 1, the directions state that the sentence is missing a comma. (The "Little Squiggles"—commas, apostrophes, and quotation marks—are popular when it comes to testing punctuation.) Remind your child that a comma denotes a pause in the sentence. Therefore, if he's having problems with this or any other "comma" question, he can try all the answer choices by saying the words to himself, pausing where the different commas should be. In this way, your child can trust his ear. Have him say this out loud:

> "We wanted to bring food [pause] camping [pause] equipment and water on our journey into the mountains."

That shouldn't sound right to anybody, since it creates a space between *camping equipment,* which is one item. Therefore, A is incorrect. Have your child repeat this process with both the original sentence in question and choice B. He should arrive at the correct choice C, which is demonstrates the proper placement of commas.

To answer question 2, your child has to know about proper nouns. You will recall how a proper noun refers to a specific person, place, or thing, and therefore is capitalized. For example, "I asked my father if I could go to the store" is not the same as "I asked Father McSwirly if I could go to the store." In the second sentence, *father* is used as a proper noun. Since it was referring to a specific person—Father McSwirly—both words are capitalized. Because Governor Wilson is a specific person, A is the right answer.

Although nothing is set in stone, Grammar questions will probably make up the largest portion of the ELA CRCT. If your child combines P.O.E. with some basic knowledge of spelling, capitalization, and punctuation rules, he should make it through these questions in good shape.

Paragraph Content and Organization

If your child is like many third graders, the idea of writing something—a paragraph, or even an essay—that will be graded is not one she looks forward to. On this part of the CRCT, tell your child:

> ***You do not need to write an essay, you just need to answer multiple-choice questions about the best way to construct an essay.***

Instead of a reading passage, Content and Organization questions are usually preceded by text that looks like this:

Donald was asked to write an essay about his summer vacation. Here is part of his first rough draft.

(1) I saw many ducks while I was there. (2) This is the story about how I spent the summer at my grandparent's farm. (3) My grandparents own a dairy farm in New York. (4) It was fun to get away from all the noise of the big city. (5) Riding horses through the fields. (6) I enjoyed spending time with my grandparents as well.

35

4. Which sentence states the main idea of the paragraph?
    A. 1
    B. 2
    C. 3
    D. 4

5. Which of the following sentences would belong in Donald's report?
    A. Many people drink milk from cows every day.
    B. Parents usually spend time with their grandparents.
    C. Humans have lived with animals for many years.
    D. It was fun to feed the chickens on the farm.

To answer question 4, it helps if your child understands the main idea of the paragraph. Does that bit of advice sound familiar? It should, since it a useful tip on the Reading CRCT questions. If your child realizes that the main idea is about spending time on a farm, sentence 2 (answer choice B) is the best answer for that question.

With the main idea of the paragraph still in mind, have your child look over question 5. Which sentence best fits in with a child spending time on a farm? Choice D, which has the words "on the farm" in it, is definitely the best answer.

Understanding the main idea of an essay is a key ingredient to answering Content and Organization questions about it.

Sentence Construction and Revision

Sentence Construction problems often revolve around the eight parts of speech (nouns, verbs, etc.), requiring your child to recognize these parts of speech and how they are used to create a sentence. Here is an example:

ENGLISH/LANGUAGE ARTS

6. What is the compound verb in the sentence below?

   Why didn't Gerald jump and avoid the baseball that the opposing pitcher threw at his feet?
   - A. threw
   - B. at his feet
   - C. the opposing pitcher
   - D. jump and avoid

Even if the word *compound* makes your child scratch his head, he could use P.O.E. on the answer choices. Which of the choices contain no verbs? If your child understands what a verb is, he should be able to cross out B and C. At this point, he could take a guess—D is the right answer.

Other Sentence Construction and Revision questions require the student to identify the types of sentences (declarative, interrogative, imperative, exclamatory), which shouldn't be too difficult to practice—you probably tell, ask, request, and excite your child every day!

Research Process/Source Materials

These questions are similar to basic obstacles that anyone doing a little research might encounter. For instance, your child might have a dictionary-related question like:

7. Look at the top of the dictionary page.

   Stumble—Stylize

   Which word can be found on this page?
   - A. stub
   - B. stubble
   - C. sturdy
   - D. stylized

Even if your child has never worked with a dictionary, question 7 is still very solvable. All she needs is a knowledge of the alphabet and the ability to not let a strange-looking question faze her. Using process of elimination on each answer choice, the only

DICTIONARY SPRINTS

This game requires one dictionary per person. Each person starts with his or her dictionary closed, and one player begins by making a statement like, "First person to find an adverb wins." Players then flip open the dictionary and scan the page until they find an entry with *adv.*, which is how a word that is an adverb is usually designated. The winner gets a point.

Other sprints could include "first person to find a word with a Latin root," or "first person to find a word with six or more definitions" or even "first person to find an entry with a synonym." Since you need to understand a dictionary in order to play the game, you can teach your child along the way, or you both can turn to the front of the dictionary and learn about all the different terminology.

one that would appear after *Stumble* but before *Stylize* is choice C, *sturdy*. B and D are traps to catch a student who wants to pick an answer that looks a lot like a word within the question.

The other prevalent type of Research question requires the student to pick the proper reference source for a question, as in the following example:

8. To find countries surrounding Lithuania, you should look in —
    A. a dictionary
    B. an almanac
    C. a newspaper
    D. an atlas

Questions like number 8 above hinge on your child's familiarity with major reference sources, such as the four answer choices listed. If your child knows what each of these sources are best used for, these questions should be fairly simple. Even if the answer to a particular question is not one of the four choices above, your child can still apply her knowledge of these reference guides and use process of elimination. In question 8, the best reference to find the countries that surround Lithuania would be an atlas (D), since atlases specialize in maps and geographic information. She could also arrive at that answer by knowing what A, B, and C are used for, and eliminate them as such.

Chapter Five   SCIENCE AND SOCIAL STUDIES

As we mentioned in the Introduction, Georgia plans to debut Science and Social Studies CRCTs in Spring 2002 in grades 3 through 8. At the time of this book's publication, little else is known about these two exams. Truthfully, until these tests are administered by the Georgia Department of Education, all discussion about the Science and Social Studies CRCTs will be mostly speculation.

But that doesn't mean we can't do some speculation and form an idea of what these tests will probably look like. It's fairly safe to say that the tests will be multiple-choice-only, with between 40 and 60 questions (plus some field-test questions on each test). Furthermore, many of the skills and tips covered in the previous chapters—such as the two-pass system, reading charts and graphs, and our friend P.O.E.—are more than applicable to the Science and Social Studies tests. Having a good grasp of the basics of history and science is, of course, essential. But many students fall into the trap of overstudying, learning minutiae that won't appear on the test. You want your child to be knowledgeable about historical events and scientific phenomena, but excessive studying would just wear him out. This isn't a good choice, so concentrate on the basics.

> **What Counts**
>
> How the Science and Social Studies CRCTs will be used to evaluate your child's learning will once again be a local decision. However, you should know that in several other U.S. states, the Science and Social Studies state-mandated exams are not as "high stakes" as the Math and English tests. The prevailing reason for this is that many believe the mastery of basic math and English skills is essential for grade promotion, but mastery of science and social studies is less critical. For this reason, while the Science and Social Studies exams are used to evaluate a student's performance, they are not tied to advancement to the next grade. Again, your local school board will determine all this some time around 2002.

In this chapter, we've provided some Science and Social Studies content areas to give you and your child an idea what "the basics" means. The content strands are from Georgia's Quality Core Curriculum, and since the CRCT is designed to test these strands, they should give you a broad but accurate idea of what information will be tested.

PARENT'S GUIDE TO THE GEORGIA CRCT FOR GRADE 3

Science CRCT

On the Science CRCT, using your head can take you a long way, so make sure your child doesn't get flustered and think there is some high-falutin' science knowledge that he must have before the test in order to do well. Consider a question about shadows. Does your child need schooling in optics and parallax to know that the longest shadows occur when the sun is lowest, and that shadows are shortest when the sun is high? The authors of this book don't even know what parallax is, but we can answer a question like this one:

> A person is standing in an open field in Athens during the summer. Sunrise is at 6:43 A.M. that day, while sunset is at 8:52 P.M. At what time will this person's shadow be the longest?
>
> A. 7:42 A.M.
> B. 9:02 P.M.
> C. 1:04 A.M.
> D. 1:04 P.M.

If your child thinks about this question, and uses common sense, she can find the right answer. B and C are incorrect because the sun will not be out, leaving only A and D. At 1:04 P.M., the sun should almost overhead, so it won't cast much of a shadow. That leaves us with A as the correct answer.

Generally speaking, there will probably be more questions involving common sense on the Science CRCT than on other subject tests. While there is usually a precise, scientific explanation for many of the questions, simply understanding the basic scientific principles and applying common sense will often work just as well.

For those of you who are skeptical about this fact, let the following story comfort you:

KAPLAN'S TEST-PREP FABLES: THE BILLIARDS BATTLE BETWEEN DR. R. WILLINGTON REMIGIUS, MATH PROFESSOR EXTRAORDINAIRE, AND NORTH DAKOTA SLIM

Normally a man who devoted all his spare time to solving mathematical problems so difficult that most people could not even look at them without having to take aspirin, Dr. R. Willington Remigius left the university early one afternoon in order to learn more about an exciting new game he had just heard about. It was called "pool," and Remigius was certain that with his math skills he could soon become the world's greatest pool player.

Arriving at a local pool hall, Dr. Remigius soon had his theory confirmed. "Why, this game is nothing more than Newton's Second Law of Physics combined with Vector Calculus!" he exclaimed, and promptly picked up a pool cue. "Who wants to play me?"

Using his knowledge of math and physics, Remigius was able to calculate precisely how much force he needed to hit the cue ball, and at what angle. He quickly won several games, and soon a crowd has gathered around his pool table. "Who has the brains to beat me at pool?" Remigius boasted.

"Ah'll play yuh, sir," drawled a lanky youth everyone knew as North Dakota Slim. Slim was so tall and thin that when he stood next to his pool cue, people couldn't tell which one was which.

The match began, and using precise calculations Remigius sank three of his balls on the first try. Slim countered, sinking four of his balls on the next turn. The match came down to a final shot on the 8 ball, and to make it Slim would have to knock the cue ball off five different bumpers, as well as the exact corner of one of the side pockets.

Remigius's head was spinning as he tried to do the math in his head, but Slim was unconcerned. He strode up to the table, and calmly hit the winning shot. "How did you do that?" asked a humbled Remigius.

"Vector calculus is vector calculus," replied North Dakota Slim. "Pool is pool."

Moral: You don't need to know the exact scientific principle of something to have a good idea of how it works.

PARENT'S GUIDE TO THE GEORGIA CRCT FOR GRADE 3

A Note about Chart Questions

Many questions on the Science CRCT contain a visual element, such as a chart or graph. This is good news, because . . .

> *answering a chart/graph question on the Science CRCT is the same as answering a chart/graph question on the Math CRCT.*

The following example illustrates this point:

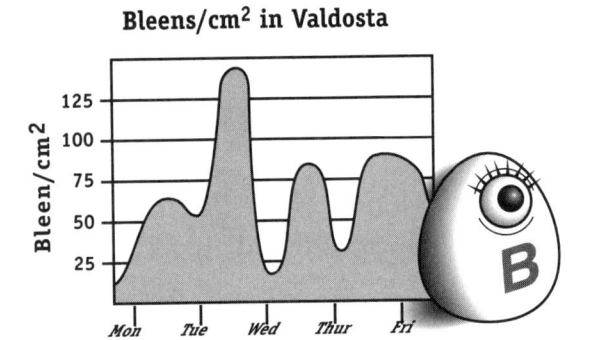

Bleens/cm² in Valdosta

How many Bleens/cm² in Valdosta were there on Tuesday?

A. 75 Bleens/cm²

B. 50 Bleens/cm²

C. 25 Bleens/cm²

D. 0 Bleens/cm²

Maybe "Bleens per cubic centimeter" is some very important scientific phenomenon that needs to be tracked, and maybe not. The point is your child can answer a question like the one above without knowing what a Bleen is. All he has to do is read the graph correctly to arrive at answer B, which is all that will be counted on this exam.

SCIENCE AND SOCIAL STUDIES

Earth Science
There is only one object your child needs to know in order to ace questions in this domain: the Earth. Earth Science questions talk about minerals, the composition of soil, volcanoes, fossils, erosion, and other things that make up our little blue planet. Still, it's important to keep in mind that your child doesn't need to be a volcanologist to know that lava is hot.

As with the other Science CRCT categories, the key to Earth Sciences is knowing the Big Picture. For instance, on a question about erosion, your child doesn't need to know high-level fluid dynamics; she just needs to understand that "water causes things to wear down, and so does exposure to wind." Students could spend a lot of hours in a library learning tons of different science facts, and while this would be good for their overall education, it's not crucial for the Science CRCT.

Chemistry
At the third-grade level, chemistry questions often involve the basic properties of matter, such as mass, buoyancy, size, texture, and color. Also, the difference between solids, liquids, and gases is an important topic.

Laboratory Safety
As its name suggests, this content strand will quiz students on proper safety procedures in the lab. Common sense will be important in this category. For instance, do you need a science degree to know that carrying acid in your jacket pocket is not a good idea?

Life Science
Life Science questions test students on how well they know the traits and habits of animals and plants. Does your child understand a basic food chain, with the little guys getting eaten by the big guys? If so, your child will do well in this section, or in corporate finance. Other Life Science problems ask about the difference between living and nonliving, and how animals and plants adapt to their environment.

Physics
Physics questions deal with the world around us. There are questions about chemical and physical changes; friction; energy; mass, force, and inertia; and simple machines like pulleys, levers, wedges, and inclined planes.

Process Skills
The ability to evaluate information properly is a key part of Process Skills. Since this information will often appear in the form of a graph, these questions boil down to nothing more than Chart/Graph problems.

Research and Reference Skills
Using research materials correctly is the basis of this category. In this respect, questions here will be identical to Research Process problems in the English/Language Arts CRCT, and should be approached using the same test-taking strategies.

Social Studies CRCT

Most of the questions on the Social Studies CRCT with deal specifically with U.S. history. However, this is a very broad topic, so having your child study all history would be beneficial but highly time-consuming. Fortunately, the GDOE has the following content domains to help you break down this test somewhat.

Information Processing

Many of these questions will have some piece of text—such as an old newspaper article—to accompany them. In essence, then, this content domain consists of mini-Reading passages followed by an Inference question. This illustrates how good test-taking strategies can work well in multiple situations.

Problem-Solving Skills

This strand is fairly vague since it covers a broad topic. In truth, every question requires problem-solving skills of some sort. Tell your child not to worry about this particular category—he would make better use of his time studying concepts in Civic Participation and Map and Globe Skills, two more manageable content strands.

Civic Participation

To put it succinctly, these problems quiz students on the various branches of government, and what their function is. For example, a question might ask where one would have to go to renew a driver's license: the Georgia Supreme Court, the Department of Transportation, or the Lottery Commission? To get the Big Picture on Democratic Process problems, your child needs to be familiar the Big Three branches of state government: Executive (president or governor), Legislative (Senate and/or House of Representatives), and Judicial (the courts).

Time and Chronology

In addition to asking questions about the history of Georgia and the United States, these questions often test whether a student understands the sequence of events in history. Because sequence is important, some questions will feature a time line, which is a boon to your child. This is because these questions do not require your child to have any previous knowledge of a specific historical event, she just simply has to interpret the events that appear on the time line.

Map and Globe Skills

Questions stemming from this content area are very easy to spot, since almost every geography-type question comes

> **GET THE WHOLE WORLD IN YOUR HANDS**
>
> To give your child some more experience with maps, play the Globe Game. Using a globe, Player 1 closes her eyes and spins the globe, while the other player names a continent, ocean, or country. The player with her eyes closed must now try to place her finger on the spinning globe at the correct location. Although Player 1 probably won't be successful, wherever her finger lands, discuss the various topographical features of that area (mountain, deserts, rivers, and so forth) so that your child learns to read maps well.

with a map. Furthermore, the key to these questions is simply reading a map properly, so make sure your child is familiar with maps and map symbols, and the Map and Globe Skills questions will practically fall off the map and into his lap.

This concludes our brief discussion of the Science and Social Studies curriculum frameworks. There will probably be charts and maps throughout the both these CRCTs—just tell your child to answer them the same way he would answer a Math chart question. There will also be times when the best way to approach a question is to apply the process of elimination. In other words, combining the techniques your child has learned in previous sections with some basic historical and scientific knowledge and a healthy dose of common sense will give him all the tools he needs to succeed on the Science CRCT and the Social Studies CRCT.

Chapter Six I GOT A WHAT?!

Your child's scores on the CRCT will be broken down into three main categories: a scaled score, an achievement level score, and a percentage subscore.

The scaled score is a number between 150 and 450, with 300 being the minimum score needed to pass each CRCT. Every student's scaled score corresponds to one of the three Achievement Levels below.

> **Internet Information**
>
> For the most up-to-date information about the CRCT, check out the Georgia Department of Education's Website at www.doe.k12.ga.us.

Achievement Level	Scaled Score
Exceeds Standard	351–450
Meets Standard	300–350
Does Not Meet Standard	150–299

The scaled scores are a more precise breakdown of the Achievement Levels. In other words, since the minimum scaled score needed to receive a Meets Standard rating in Math is 300, a child who scores 310 and a child who scores a 340 will both receive this ranking, but the second child's test score was better than the first child's score.

In addition to the scaled score and Achievement Level ranking, your child will also receive a percentage score in the Reading, Mathematics, and other content categories. These are used to report how well your child performed on all those types of questions we outlined throughout the book. If, for example, your child receives a 75 percent on the Geometry and Measurement subscore, that means she answered three fourths of those questions correctly.

While a low score can be a cause for concern, it should not necessarily be considered an indication that your child is lagging far behind in her studies and that her education so far has been worthless. Be sure to discuss her scores with the person who is very knowledgeable about your child's ability as a student: her teacher. Your child's teacher will provide a better, more complete overview of your child's academic standing than a single numerical score from a standardized test. It is important that parents keep these scores in perspective.

In terms of how Georgia's Criterion-Referenced Competency Tests will be scored, this is the end of the story. However, it should be noted that in this case, the phrase "end of story" only means "end of discussion on how your child scored on the standardized test." Your child has about a decade of schooling ahead of her. This test should be seen for what it is: an interesting checkpoint along a very long highway. Some students who scored at the lowest level on this test will go on to graduate from prestigious universities with advanced degrees, while other students who scored at the top will struggle to finish high school. Your child's scores simply highlight where she needs improvement. And the best person available to make sure your child receives that improvement is currently reading the last sentence of this chapter.

Chapter Seven MATH AND READING PRACTICE

This chapter contains practice multiple-choice questions for you to work through with your child. Refer to page 53 for the correct answers.

Math Review Questions

The bar graph shows the results of a favorite color survey at Willkie school.

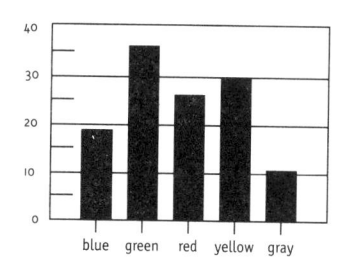

1. Which color was the favorite color of fewer than 15 students?
   A. blue
   B. red
   C. yellow
   D. gray

2. How much string is needed to go all the way around the poster?
   A. 35 ft
   B. 24 ft
   C. 17 ft
   D. 12 ft

3. Which number has a 2 in the thousands place?
   A. 72,563
   B. 56,372
   C. 63,725
   D. 27,256

GO ON

49

4. The children's museum has 32 pieces of art. Some of the pieces are paintings, and the rest are statues. Let *p* represent the number of paintings in the museum, and let *s* represent the number of sculptures. Which of the following expressions shows how many paintings there are in the children's museum?

   A. $s + p$
   B. $32 - p$
   C. $32 - s$
   D. $32 + s - p$

5. The library has 35 science books, 62 nature books, 33 history books, and 20 fiction books. If the library trades all of its history books to another library in exchange for an equal amount of nature books in return, what will be the total number of nature books in the library then?

   A. 62
   B. 82
   C. 95
   D. 97

GO ON

Reading Review Questions

The Third-Grade Talent Show

Laura Zegman was looking forward to seeing her younger brothers' talent show. It was the first talent show ever for the twins, and they had worked on their juggling act to prepare for this evening.

It was about time for the talent show to start. Laura's father handed her a piece of paper as she sat down next to her parents. "It's a schedule of the talent show."

BRAZELTON ELEMENTARY SCHOOL PRESENTS

The Third Annual Third-Grade Talent Show

Thursday, March 23, at 6:30 in the Gym

Fruit and punch will be served in the cafeteria after the show.

Schedule of Acts

6:30	Introduction	Principal Ertel Hall
6:45	Song, "We Are the World"	Jacqueline Biedenfeld
6:50	Ballet, "Swan Lake"	Pete Szcerbiak
7:00	The Juggling Zegmans	Ernst and Mike Zegman
7:10	Piano, "21st Century Chopsticks"	Portia Heimdall
7:30	Magic Act, "The Vanishing Snail"	Walter Ross
7:40	Song, "Camptown Races"	Joanie Iber
7:55	Closing Remarks	Principal Ertel Hall
8:00	End of Talent Show	

The talent show performers would like to thank the following people for their help in making this show possible:

- Ms. Claudia Baba for helping set up the stage.
- Ms. Alexis Biedenfeld for loaning her favorite snail for the Magic Act.
- Mr. Mark Kossover for helping with the lighting.
- All our families for giving us their support.

PARENT'S GUIDE TO THE GEORGIA CRCT FOR GRADE 3

1. How did Laura feel about going to the talent show?
   - A. scared
   - B. puzzled
   - C. interested
   - D. disappointed

2. If the schedule is correct, which act will probably take longer than any other?
   - A. the juggling
   - B. the singing
   - C. the ballet dancing
   - D. the piano playing

3. What will happen just after the talent show ends?
   - A. Fruit will be served.
   - B. Schedules will be handed out.
   - C. The stage will be set up.
   - D. The principal will make an introduction.

4. Why did Laura attend the talent show?
   - A. She wanted to see the magic act.
   - B. She wanted to see the juggling act.
   - C. She likes fruit and punch.
   - D. Her parents made her attend.

5. This story is mostly about how Laura —
   - A. sat down next to her mother and father
   - B. liked to watch juggling at the talent show
   - C. helped her brothers practice their act
   - D. learned about the acts in the talent show

ANSWERS

Math Review Questions

1. D
2. B
3. A
4. C
5. C

Reading Review Questions

1. C
2. D
3. A
4. B
5. D

How Did We Do? Grade Us.

Thank you for choosing a Kaplan book. Your comments and suggestions are very useful to us. Please answer the following questions to assist us in our continued development of high-quality resources to meet your needs.

The title of the Kaplan book I read was: _____

My name is: _____

My address is: _____
_____

My e-mail address is: _____

What overall grade would you give this book?	Ⓐ	Ⓑ	Ⓒ	Ⓓ	Ⓕ
How relevant was the information to your goals?	Ⓐ	Ⓑ	Ⓒ	Ⓓ	Ⓕ
How comprehensive was the information in this book?	Ⓐ	Ⓑ	Ⓒ	Ⓓ	Ⓕ
How accurate was the information in this book?	Ⓐ	Ⓑ	Ⓒ	Ⓓ	Ⓕ
How easy was the book to use?	Ⓐ	Ⓑ	Ⓒ	Ⓓ	Ⓕ
How appealing was the book's design?	Ⓐ	Ⓑ	Ⓒ	Ⓓ	Ⓕ

What were the book's strong points? _____

How could this book be improved? _____

Is there anything that we left out that you wanted to know more about?

Would you recommend this book to others? ☐ YES ☐ NO

Other comments: _____
_____
_____

Do we have permission to quote you? ☐ YES ☐ NO

Thank you for your help.
Please tear out this page and mail it to:

    Managing Editor
    Kaplan, Inc.
    888 Seventh Avenue
    New York, NY 10106

KAPLAN

Thanks!